WITHDRAWN

KID CONCOCTIONS

BIBLICAL

PROPORTIONS

John E. & Danita Thomas

B&H
PUBLISHING GROUP
Nashville, Tennessee

Copyright © 2007 by John E. and Danita Thomas
All rights reserved.
Printed in the United States of America

Thirteen-digit ISBN: 978-0-8054-4447-6

Published by B&H Publishing Group, Nashville, Tennessee

Dewey Decimal Classification: 372.5
Subject Heading: CREATIVE ACTIVITIES \ HANDICRAFT

No part of this book may be reproduced mechanically, electronically, photocopying or any other means without prior written permission from the publisher, except for book reviews.

Kid Concoctions™ is a trademark of Kid Concoctions Company.

Authors are represented by the literary agency of Nashville Agency,
P. O. Box 110909, Nashville, Tennessee 37222.

CREDITS:
Cover art design: Robert Durr
Cover photography: Jack Dragga
Illustrations: Robb Durr and Zachariah Durr

Authors' Web site: www.kidconcoctions.com
Publisher's Web site: www.BHPublishingGroup.com

All Scripture quotations are from the Holy Bible, New International Version (NIV),
copyright © 1973, 1978, 1984 by International Bible Society.

Notice: The information in this book is true, complete, and accurate to the best of our knowledge. All suggestions and recommendations are made without guarantees on the part of the authors or the publisher. The authors and publisher disclaim all liability incurred in connection with the use of this information.

1 2 3 4 5 6 7 8 9 10   11 10 09 08 07

FOND DU LAC PUBLIC LIBRARY

5.5
64K

Dedications

We would like to dedicate this book to our children:
Kyle, Kalie, Kellen, and Christian who inspire us
each day to keep concocting!

"May you live a life full of love, faith, happiness,
and creativity we inspire to share."

Acknowledgments

We would like to thank the children, parents, grandparents, educators, and all the others who have supported Kid Concoctions and helped it grow into more than we ever dreamed possible.

Other titles by John and Danita Thomas:

The Ultimate Book of Kid Concoctions
(ISBN 10: 0-8054-4443-2 / ISBN 13: 978-0-8054-4443-8)

The Ultimate Book of Kid Concoctions 2
(ISBN 10: 0-8054-4444-0 / ISBN 13: 978-0-8054-4444-5)

Kid Concoctions and Contraptions
(ISBN 10: 0-8054-4446-7 / ISBN 13: 978-0-8054-4446-9)

The Ultimate Book of Holiday Kid Concoctions
(ISBN 10: 0-8054-4445-9 / ISBN 13: 978-0-8054-4445-2)

Foreword

Kid Concoctions of Biblical Proportions is the fifth book in the Kid Concoctions series. We are very excited because this is the first book we have written specifically for families of faith. In this book we share with you many brand-new projects, along with some of our all-time most popular ideas. For every project we have included a corresponding scriptural truth to help your children grow spiritually.

Kid Concoctions has been embraced by parents and teachers for many years because the books help children learn and create while they are having fun. Now in addition to basic math, science, and life skills, children will also learn biblical lessons, practical spiritual truths, and instruction for living as a child of God.

When we first began Kid Concoctions more than a decade ago, we tested each new project with the children in our Sunday school class. This quickly became their favorite part of the class. Each week we presented a project along with our weekly Scripture verse to make learning a little more fun. The proportion of children who remembered the verse after these creative play sessions was nearly 100 percent! Now that Kid Concoctions has found success in the mainstream market, we are excited to return to our Sunday school roots.

As Christian parents, we believe that one of our most important tasks is to impart to our children a strong foundation of God's Word and His promises for each of us. We joyfully share these fun projects and scriptural truths with you in hopes they will bless you and the children you inspire.

May God bless you and your family.

John E. Thomas & Danita Thomas

CONTENTS

Treasure Stones 10

Promise of the Rainbow Paint 11

Fruit of the Spirit Dough 12

Dog and Cat Treats 13

Sparkle Lamp 14

Mini Garden of Eden 15

Grass Hair Guy 16

Fizzle Stones 17

Storm in a Bottle 18

Power of Prayer Rain Stick 19

Gooey Creation Gunk 20

Bubbling Peace Paint 21

Miracle Art Board 22

Phony Spill 23

Word Cannon 24

Marble Paint 26

Heavenly Cloud Paint 27

Romans Ice Cream 28

Scents of Joy 29

Resurrection Sand Eggs 30

Honey Lip Balm 32

"No Worry" Bird Cookies 33

Edible Ocean in a Bag 34

Friendship Stone 35

Hydro Jet Ark 36

Living Basket 38

Color-Change Bath Salts 39

Sparkling Glitter Candles 40

Flower Transfers 41

Living Words 42

Creation Sand Plaques 43

Splongee Ball of Virtues 44

Heavenly Treasures Bottle 45

Divine Dryer Lint Clay 46

Water Balloon Yo-Yo 47

World's Best Bubbles 48

Bubble Paint 49

Scripture Sidewalk Chalk 50

Super Sidewalk Paint 51

David's Slingshot Flyer 52

Moses' Miracle Muck 53

Cinnamon Heart Ornaments 54

Washable Window Art 55

Jiggle Orange Slices 56

Super Bubble Slime 57

Ten Commandments Paint Pens 58

Shower Time Paints 60

Beautiful-in-Time Marbleizing 61

Holiday Peppermint Wreaths 62

Shake-and-Make Slushy 63

Surprise Soaps 64

Spaghetti Ice Cream Sundae 65

Growing Eggheads 66

Funny-Face Toast 67

Heavenly Cloud Marshmallows 68

God's Compass 69

Stained Glass Lamp 70

Chocolate Smooches 71

Popcorn Treasure Balls 72

Pathway Lanterns 73

Surging Sea Lamp 74

Manna Dessert 75

Index 77–78

Adult supervision is recommended for all projects and recipes, especially those using a stove, oven, microwave, or glue gun. Some ingredients used in these recipes, such as Borax, plaster of Paris, and quick dry cement should be handled only by adults wearing protective gloves.

TREASURE STONES

Treasure Stones illustrate how man looks at the outward appearance but God looks at the heart. This is a wonderful project for a birthday party, scavenger hunt, or a Sunday school class.

WHAT YOU WILL NEED:

Treasures: Plastic jewelry, coins, small plastic toys, erasers, etc.
1 cup flour
1 cup used coffee grounds
1/2 cup salt
1/4 cup sand
3/4 cup water

HOW TO CONCOCT IT:

1. Mix all dry ingredients together in a medium bowl.
2. Slowly add water and knead until the mixture is the consistency of cookie dough.
   If the dough is too sticky or wet, add more flour. If the dough is too dry, add more water.
3. Break off a piece of dough and roll it into the size of a baseball.
4. Make a hole in the center of the ball big enough to hide treasures in.
5. Fill the hole with treasures and seal with some extra dough.
6. Place the Treasure Stones on a cookie sheet and bake in the over at 150 degrees for
   15 to 20 minutes.

Man looks at the outward appearance, but the LORD [God] looks at the heart. (1 Samuel 16:7)

CONCOCTION TIPS & IDEAS:

◆ Hide the Treasure Stones in your backyard and give everyone a treasure map to have the ultimate treasure hunt.
◆ Break the stone open piece by piece. This is what God does for us when we find Him. He slowly takes away the old and ugly stone, uncovering the treasures of our heart. Maybe the stone is there because someone hurt our feelings, and over time the hurt turned to anger, or because we did bad things that we felt terrible about later. All of these things can make us feel bad about ourselves and cause the shell surrounding our heart to turn cold and harden.

PROMISE OF THE RAINBOW PAINT

This project will allow you to paint a beautiful rainbow in one stroke. It also reminds us of God's promise to Noah and all mankind.

WHAT YOU WILL NEED:

3-inch sponge brush

Paper

Food coloring (red, yellow, and blue)

HOW TO CONCOCT IT:

1. Wet the sponge and squeeze to remove excess water.
2. Squeeze several drops of food coloring on the sponge to make a vertical row of red, yellow, and blue on the tip of the sponge.
3. Paint with a sponge on a large sheet of paper to create Rainbow Paint pictures.

CONCOCTION TIPS & IDEAS:

◆ Use Rainbow Paint to create wrapping paper, gift bags, greeting cards, banners, and pictures.
◆ While making rainbow prints on the paper, share the story of why God sent the rainbow—His promise to mankind. Share the story of Noah and his obedience to God and the reward we all receive for obeying and trusting God.

"I will remember my covenant between me and you and all living creatures of every kind. Never again will the waters become a flood to destroy all life. Whenever the rainbow appears in the clouds, I will see it and remember the everlasting covenant between God and all living creatures of every kind on the earth."
(Genesis 9:15–16)

FRUIT OF THE SPIRIT DOUGH

This fruit-scented dough can be molded into shapes, illustrating the different fruits of the Spirit that God wants to grow in each of us.

WHAT YOU WILL NEED:

2 1/4 cups flour

1 cup salt

2 Tbs. unsweetened powdered drink mix

4 Tbs. cooking oil

1 cup water

HOW TO CONCOCT IT:

1. Combine flour, salt, and powdered drink mix in a large bowl.
2. Stir in cooking oil and water.
3. Continue stirring until mixture is the consistency of bread dough.
4. Remove dough from bowl and knead on a floured surface for 2 to 3 minutes until firm.

CONCOCTION TIPS & IDEAS:

◆ Store Fruit of the Spirit Dough in an airtight container or plastic ziplock bag.

◆ This project is a great way to let children experience fruit of another kind. The fruits of the Spirit grow in us when we are living in ways that are obedient and pleasing to God.

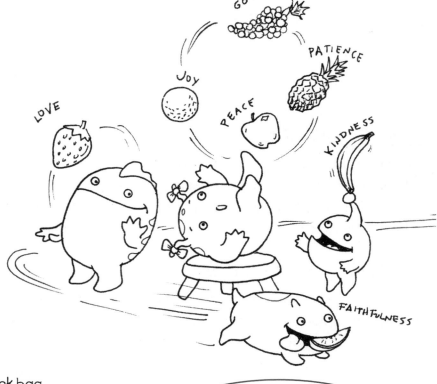

But the fruit of the Spirit is love, joy, peace, patience, kindness, goodness, faithfulness, gentleness and self-control. (Galations 5:22–23)

DOG AND CAT TREATS

God is pleased when we care for and nurture our pets. Your dog or cat will also be pleased when they dine on these gourmet treats.

WHAT YOU WILL NEED:

2 cups whole wheat flour
1/4 cup cornmeal
1/2 cup Parmesan cheese
1 medium egg
1 cup water

HOW TO CONCOCT IT:

1. Mix all ingredients except 1/4 cup of the Parmesan cheese. Knead until thoroughly mixed.
2. Roll the dough mixture into 3-inch, pencil-size treat sticks. Roll the treat sticks in the remaining Parmesan cheese.
3. Twist the treat sticks 3 to 4 times. Then place the treats on an ungreased cookie sheet and bake at 350 degrees for 25 to 30 minutes.
4. Store treats in an airtight container. One batch makes 18 to 20 small treats.

CONCOCTION TIPS & IDEAS:

◆ Use cookie cutters to create treats in different shapes and sizes.
◆ Knead in 8 to 10 drops of food coloring to add color to your treats.
◆ When making the treats, talk about being gentle and kind to animals and why it is important to remember that this commandment comes from God.

A righteous man cares for the needs of his animal, but the kindest acts of the wicked are cruel.
(Proverbs 12:10)

SPARKLE LAMP

Just as light from the Sparkle Lamp shows us the way to walk in the dark, the Bible shows us the way to walk through life.

WHAT YOU WILL NEED:

Glass baby food jar (clean with the label removed)

White glue

Paintbrush

Salt

Stickers

HOW TO CONCOCT IT:

1. Press stickers on the outside of the baby food jar.
2. Paint over the stickers and the entire outside of the jar with a thin layer of white glue.
3. Sprinkle a generous amount of salt over the wet glue on the outside of the jar.
4. Let the jar dry overnight, and then place a tea candle inside of the jar.

CONCOCTION TIPS & IDEAS:

◆ Instead of using stickers, glue pictures from magazines and photos on the Sparkle Lamp.
◆ The meaning of the Scripture below is that God's Word, the Bible, is full of directions and instructions about how we should live our lives as Christians. God's directions and instructions will guide us to live a life pleasing to Him and rich with His blessing.

Your word is a lamp to my feet and a light for my path.
(Psalm 119:105)

MINI GARDEN OF EDEN

God has given us the gift of fruits and vegetables to eat. The Mini Garden of Eden teaches responsibility for taking care of these blessings.

WHAT YOU WILL NEED:

Clear plastic 2-liter bottle
Seeds
Peat moss
Flowerpot
Pebbles or small rocks

HOW TO CONCOCT IT:

1. Have an adult cut the plastic bottle in half. Use the top half of the bottle for your Mini Garden of Eden.
2. Place a handful of pebbles or small rocks in the bottom of the flowerpot, then add peat moss and seeds.
3. Place the top half of the bottle over the pot and place your Mini Garden of Eden in a sunny spot.
4. Water your garden a few times a week or when the peat moss gets dry.

CONCOCTION TIPS & IDEAS:

◆ Use brightly colored paints to decorate the flowerpot with Scriptures and illustrations of things that may have been found in the Garden of Eden.
◆ As we explore nature, we see the beauty and miracle of God's creation. God not only made us brilliant, but He provided us with just the right foods we need to survive and thrive.

The LORD God took the man and put him in the Garden of Eden to work it and take care of it. (Genesis 2:15)

GRASS HAIR GUY

Imagine trying to keep track of each piece of grass hair on your Grass Hair Guy. God actually knows and loves each of us so much. He knows every hair on our heads!

WHAT YOU WILL NEED:

Nylon stocking

6 Tbs. potting soil

2 Tbs. grass seed

Plastic yogurt container (single-serving size)

2 google eyes

Glue

Waterproof markers or fabric paint

Water

HOW TO CONCOCT IT:

1. Cut a 4-inch long piece of nylon stocking, including the toe. Spoon the grass seed into the stocking.

2. Pour the potting soil into the stocking until you have a ball of soil that is about 2 inches in diameter.

3. Tie a knot in the stocking so the soil will hold its ball shape. (Do not cut the tail off the stocking.)

4. Glue a set of google eyes on your grass head and then draw a nose or mouth using water-proof markers or fabric paint.

   (Let the glue and paint completely dry before continuing to the next step.)

5. Fill the yogurt container 1/2 full with water. Soak your grass head in water until it is completely wet, then place your Grass Hair Guy on top of the yogurt container, making sure the nylon tail sits in the water. Check the water level in the plastic yogurt container daily.

And even the very hairs of your head are all numbered.
(Matthew 10:30)

CONCOCTION TIPS & IDEAS:

◆ Use construction paper, glue, and markers to decorate the yogurt container and create a body and clothes for your Grass Hair Guy.

◆ Keeping track and knowing each piece of grass hair may seem easy at first, but it becomes very difficult.

FIZZLE STONES

These awesome stones dissolve to reveal secret surprises inside, just as God reveals the person inside us as we grow to know Him more and more.

WHAT YOU WILL NEED:

1/4 cup baking soda
4 cups white vinegar
Small toys or plastic jewels
4 Tbs. water
Large bowl (clear works best)

HOW TO CONCOCT IT:

1. Mix baking soda and water together in a small bowl
   until a stiff dough is formed. If the dough is too moist, add more baking soda; if it is too dry, add more water.
2. Make a stone by molding the dough around a small toy or plastic jewel. (Roll the stone in baking soda if it is too moist.) Let the stone
   dry overnight.
3. Drop the Fizzle Stone into a clear bowl filled with vinegar.
4. Watch as the stone begins to fizzle and reveal its secret treasure.

CONCOCTION TIPS & IDEAS:

◆ Try coloring the baking soda with a few drops of food coloring to create
  multicolored stones.
◆ Just like the stone that seems to bubble with life while revealing a new creation, God
  creates a new and wonderful person in each of us as we accept Him and allow Him to come
  into our hearts and our lives.

If any-
one is in Christ, he is a new
creation; the old has gone,
the new has come!
(2 Corinthians 5:17)

STORM IN A BOTTLE

This fun wave toy is a great illustration of how Jesus calmed the storm.

WHAT YOU WILL NEED:

1 clear plastic 16 oz. soda bottle with a cap
12 oz. baby oil
Food coloring
4 oz. water
Funnel

HOW TO CONCOCT IT:

1. Mix 4 to 6 drops of blue food coloring and water together in a cup and then pour into the bottle using a funnel.
2. Using the funnel, pour baby oil into the bottle until it is full.
3. Screw the cap on the bottle tightly. Slowly tilt the Storm in a Bottle right to left and watch as the waves crash against the sides of the bottle.

CONCOCTION TIPS & IDEAS:

◆ Experiment by using bottles of different shapes and sizes. You can also decorate the bottle with various stickers.
◆ It should build our faith when we hear stories about how Jesus calmed the storms, healed the sick, and performed many miracles while here on earth. He cares for each of us and still watches over all who believe in Him.

He replied, "You of little faith, why are you so afraid?" Then he got up and rebuked the winds and the waves, and it was completely calm. (Matthew 8:26)

POWER OF PRAYER RAIN STICK

As you hear the sound that the Prayer Rain Stick makes, remember that the strength of prayer is more powerful than most people could ever imagine.

WHAT YOU WILL NEED:

Heavy cardboard mailing tube

2 plastic caps or duct tape to seal the tube

Nails

Hammer

Seeds, rice, or dried beans

Adhesive-backed shelf paper, wrapping paper, fabric, paint, or ribbon

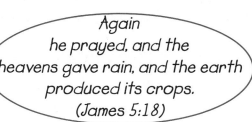

HOW TO CONCOCT IT:

1. Have an adult hammer nails into the mailing tube 1/8-inch apart, using the spiral seam of the cardboard tube as a guide.
2. Seal one end of the tube with a cap or tape.
3. Add several handfuls of seeds, rice, or dried beans to the tube.
4. Decorate your Power of Prayer Rain Stick with shelf paper, wrapping paper, fabric, paint, or ribbon.

CONCOCTION TIPS & IDEAS:

◆ Use your Power of Prayer Rain Stick as a musical instrument. Shake it and twist it while singing and praising God.

◆ God hears each of our prayers and it is important for us pray to Him often. It is good to give Him thanks and praise during our prayers, instead of always just asking things from Him. God loves each of us, and our prayers are heard by Him.

Again he prayed, and the heavens gave rain, and the earth produced its crops.
(James 5:18)

GOOEY CREATION GUNK

This project transforms two formless liquids into a solid, just as God created and transformed the formless and empty earth into His glorious creation.

WHAT YOU WILL NEED:

Solution A

    1 cup water

    1 cup white glue

    2 Tbs. poster paint or 7 to 10 drops food coloring

Solution B

    1 1/3 cups warm water

    4 tsp. Borax laundry booster

HOW TO CONCOCT IT:

1. Mix ingredients in Solution A together in a medium bowl.
2. In a second medium bowl, mix the ingredients in Solution B together until the Borax is completely dissolved.
3. Slowly pour Solution A into Solution B. (DO NOT MIX TOGETHER!)
4. Gently roll Solution A around in Solution B 4 to 5 times.
5. Lift Solution A out of Solution B and knead for 2 to 3 minutes.
6. Store Gooey Creation Gunk in an airtight container or plastic ziplock bag.

By the seventh day God had finished the work he had been doing; so on the seventh day he rested from all his work.
(Genesis 2:2)

CONCOCTION TIPS & IDEAS:

◆ Add 2 Tbs. of glow-in-the-dark paint instead of food coloring or poster paint to create glowing Gooey Creation Gunk.

◆ God created the earth and all living plants and creatures—all in just six days! On the seventh day He rested and declared this day holy.

BUBBLING PEACE PAINT

This concoction begins by overflowing and erupting out of control and then calms into a peaceful watercolor paint, reminding us that we can be more when we are calm and under control.

WHAT YOU WILL NEED:

2 tsp. clear liquid dish detergent

3 Tbs. water

1/4 cup powdered tempera paint or poster paint

HOW TO CONCOCT IT:

1. Mix clear liquid dish detergent, water, and paint together in a small, shallow bowl. If you are using concentrated dish detergent, 1 or 2 more Tbs. of water may be necessary.
2. Using a straw, gently blow into the paint mixture until a dome of bubbles forms. (DO NOT DRINK IT!)
3. Capture bubble prints by placing a piece of paper on top of the bubble dome.
4. Repeat the process, using several different colors of Bubbling Peace Paint.

CONCOCTION TIPS & IDEAS:

◆ Use your Bubbling Peace Paint to create photo frames, stationery, greeting cards, lunch bags, gift bags, party invitations, wrapping paper, and more.

◆ When we react to our family and friends with angry and hurtful words, nothing good comes of it. God's Word tells us that when we remain patient, controlled, and calm, this will quiet the fight.

A gentle answer turns away wrath, but a harsh word stirs up anger.
(Proverbs 15:1)

MIRACLE ART BOARD

Just as God turns darkness into light, the magic art board allows young artists to draw on a dark-colored board and reveal a rainbow of color. Erase it and start all over again.

WHAT YOU WILL NEED:

1 gallon-size plastic ziplock bag
8 x 10 photo mat
1/2 cup washable black poster paint
8 1/2 x 11 sheet of paper
White glue
Crayons and/or markers
Optional stickers

HOW TO CONCOCT IT:

1. Pour 1/2 cup of washable black poster paint into a gallon-size plastic ziplock bag.
2. Squeeze all of the air out of the bag and then seal the bag.
3. Place the bag over a multicolored sheet of paper. (You can color a piece of white paper with crayons or markers—lighter colors work best.)
4. Mount bag and paper in between an inexpensive cardboard photo mat and glue together.

CONCOCTION TIPS & IDEAS:

◆ Decorate the photo mat with crayons, markers, or stickers. You can even decorate it by writing on the frame your name or favorite Scripture.
◆ Just as our fingers push back the darkness on our Miracle Art Board to reveal the light and beautiful color, God is faithful to turn the darkness in our lives into light and hope.

My God turns my darkness into light.
(Psalm 18:28)

PHONY SPILL

This project is a practical joke and is not what it appears to be. Sometimes what seems good can be bad and what seems bad can be good. God helps us discern the difference between what is good and what is bad, what is real and what is not.

WHAT YOU WILL NEED:

1/2 cup white glue
1 Tbs. poster paint
Paper cup
Nonstick foil or wax paper

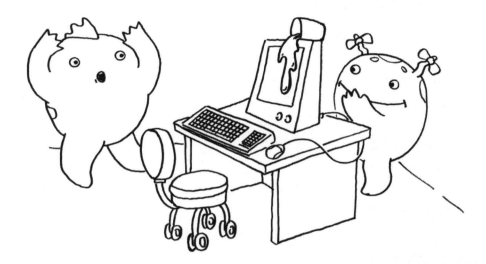

HOW TO CONCOCT IT:

1. Mix the glue and paint together in a small bowl.
2. Pour the mixture into the paper cup.
3. Lay the paper cup on its side on top of a large sheet of nonstick foil or wax paper. This will form the Phony Spill.
4. Let the spill dry for 1 to 2 days, or until completely dry. If the glue is too thick, the spill will take a long time to dry.
5. Slowly peel the spill and cup off the foil or wax paper.
6. Phony Spill should be placed on a washable, smooth, hard surface—never on fabric or carpet.

CONCOCTION TIPS & IDEAS:

◆ Be creative by making different types of spills including coffee, chocolate syrup, nail polish, and ketchup-bottle spills.
◆ Discernment is a gift God can give us when we pray to Him and ask for it. It is the ability and wisdom to know the difference between what is good or bad even when sometimes it is hard to know on our own.

I am your servant; give me discernment that I may understand your statutes.
(Psalm 119:125)

WORD CANNON

The Word Cannon shoots ping-pong balls inscribed with a Bible verse, illustrating that God's Word is more powerful than evil.

WHAT YOU WILL NEED:

2 toilet paper tubes
Tape
Plastic wrap
1 rubber band
2 paper clips
Felt-tip marker
Ping-pong balls

HOW TO CONCOCT IT:

1. Cut one toilet paper tube lengthwise.
2. Put the toilet paper tube back together with tape, making sure it is small enough to fit inside the other tube.
3. Tape plastic wrap on one end of the narrow tube. Place the smaller tube inside the larger uncut tube.
4. Place a paper clip on each end of the tube directly across from each other.
5. Attach one end of the rubber band to each of the paper clips.
6. Use a felt-tip marker to write the Word of God on each ping-pong ball.
7. Place the ping-pong ball inside the tube and pull the inner tube back and release it to launch the ball.

You, dear children, are from God . . . because the one who is in you is greater than the one who is in the world.
(1 John 4:4)

CONCOCTION TIPS & IDEAS:

◆ Set up a pyramid of toilet paper tubes with words that describe the things God wants us to avoid–hate, fear, strife, anger, sadness, division, judgment, and evil.
◆ The words on the ping-pong balls can be the opposite words of those on the tubes. God's Words tell us that we can be victorious against the enemy. These can be words that remind us of the victory we have in knowing God–love, trust, peace, patience, hope, unity, and forgiveness.

cut inside tube
lengthways

Plastic Wrap

tape to
hold plastic
wrap

Tape

LOVE

Rubber Bands

Paper Clips

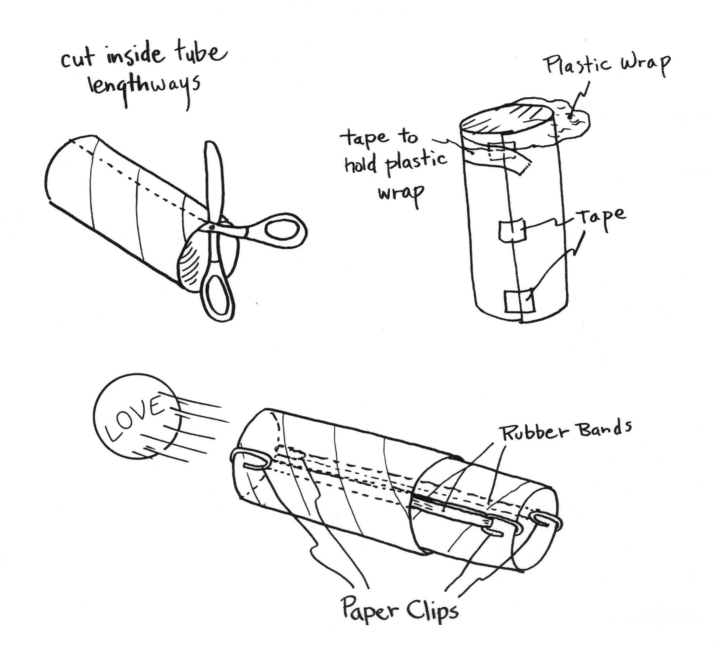

MARBLE PAINT

This fun project challenges us to roll marbles in a straight line to create beautiful works of art. It helps each of us remember how God helps us stay on a straight path.

WHAT YOU WILL NEED:

Marbles
2 Tbs. washable kids' paint
Plastic cup
Large shallow pan or box
Paper

HOW TO CONCOCT IT:

1. Pour the paint into the plastic cup.
2. Gently drop 3 or 4 marbles into the paint.
3. Place a sheet of paper inside the pan or box.
4. Spoon the paint-covered marbles out of the plastic cup and into the pan.
5. Tilt the pan or box side to side to create a Marble Paint design. Let the paint dry before handling the paper.

CONCOCTION TIPS & IDEAS:

◆ Use different colors of paint on the same sheet of paper to create interesting designs. Try using Marble Paint to create greeting cards, wrapping paper, and stationery.

◆ As we roll the marbles across the paper in the pan or box, some of the lines are straight and some are not. God will tell us, as we keep Him constantly in our thoughts, how to keep our paths straight in life. He will help us remain pure, straight, and focused on living a life pleasing to Him.

In all your ways acknowledge him, and he will make your paths straight. (Proverbs 3:6)

HEAVENLY CLOUD PAINT

Heavenly Cloud Paint can be used to create unique 3-D puffy paintings that resemble the clouds God has placed in the sky.

WHAT YOU WILL NEED:

1 cup white glue
1 cup white shaving cream
Paintbrush

HOW TO CONCOCT IT:

1. Mix the shaving cream and glue together in a small bowl.
2. Let the mixture set for 2 minutes.
3. Use a paintbrush to paint with Heavenly Cloud Paint.
   (Works best with dark-colored paper.)

CONCOCTION TIPS & IDEAS:

◆ Add 2 Tbs. of glow-in-the-dark paint or 4 to 6 drops of food coloring to add interest to your Heavenly Cloud Paint. You can use stencils of clouds to create scenes on your works of art.

◆ As we create beautiful puffy clouds, or each time we simply look up to the clouds in the sky, we are reminded that God takes care of the earth and His children by providing us clouds and rain.

*He covers the sky with clouds; he supplies the earth with rain and makes grass grow on the hills.
(Psalm 147:8)*

ROMANS ICE CREAM

With this project a few plain-tasting kitchen items work together to create delicious old-fashioned ice cream. This is just like the way God works with the "ingredients" of your life. Things that are simple, plain, and maybe even unappealing can become amazing when God brings them all together.

WHAT YOU WILL NEED:

2 Tbs. sugar

1 cup half-and-half or whipping cream

1/2 tsp. vanilla extract

6 Tbs. rock salt

1 pint-size plastic ziplock bag

1 gallon-size plastic ziplock bag

HOW TO CONCOCT IT:

1. Fill the gallon-size bag half full with ice and add rock salt.
2. Pour all remaining ingredients into the pint-size bag and seal, leaving as little air in the bag as possible.
3. Place the pint-size bag inside of the gallon bag, then seal the gallon-size bag.
4. Shake the bag 5 to 8 minutes. Then open the smaller bag and enjoy!

CONCOCTION TIPS & IDEAS:

◆ Make chocolate ice cream by eliminating the sugar and adding 2 to 3 Tbs. chocolate syrup to the half-and-half or whipping cream.

◆ Try topping your ice cream with fresh fruit or candy sprinkles.

◆ Just like the ice cream, God takes the simple things in our lives—those that are good (like the sugar in the ice cream) and those that aren't so good (like the bitter-tasting salt)— and uses them all for good. He makes us into a better person by using all the situations we go through in our lives to make us into the person He created us to be.

And we know that in all things God works for the good of those who love him. (Romans 8:28)

SCENTS OF JOY

Create your own perfume and cologne with this recipe. God tells us that loving advice from a close friend is sweet and pleasing like perfume. God gives us many blessings through the gift of good friends.

WHAT YOU WILL NEED:

2 Tbs. rubbing alcohol

1 Tbs. grated lemon peel. You can also use orange peel, cloves, vanilla bean, mint leaves, or rose petals in any combination. This is the base scent for your fragrance, so be creative!

1 plastic 35 mm-film container with snap on lid (unused or well-washed)

HOW TO CONCOCT IT:

1. Place the grated lemon peel into the plastic film container.
2. Pour rubbing alcohol on top of the lemon peel.
3. Place the lid securely on the film container and shake.
4. Let the mixture set for several days, shaking at least once a day.
5. The perfume/cologne is ready to wear when it smells like the scent you created and no longer like alcohol.

CONCOCTION TIPS & IDEAS:

◆ Decorate the film container using markers or stickers. Give your fragrances different names.

◆ Making these scents together with a friend can be a great way to celebrate your friendship. It is good to have friends who share your love and trust in God.

◆ God can use our friends to help us make choices that please and honor Him. Sometimes our friends can help us see things we are doing that may be wrong, even when we don't see it ourselves.

Perfume and incense bring joy to the heart, and the pleasantness of one's friend springs from his earnest counsel. (Proverbs 27:9)

RESURRECTION SAND EGGS

Learn this story of Jesus' resurrection by making and breaking open these unique Resurrection Sand Eggs. This is a great way to learn more about Jesus' journey.

WHAT YOU WILL NEED:

2 cups sand

1 cup cornstarch

1 1/2 cups of water

12 plastic eggs

1 old saucepan

Story items:

1. Plastic leaf
2. Small cloth with perfume
3. Salad crouton
4. Silver coin (dime)
5. Small metal or plastic cross
6. Thorny branch
7. Dice
8. Nail
9. Small piece of sponge
10. Whole cloves
11. Small rock

HOW TO CONCOCT IT:

1. Combine sand, cornstarch, and water together in an old saucepan.
2. Have an adult cook the mixture over medium heat while constantly stirring. Eventually the mixture will turn into a stiff clay. Let the sand cool completely before handling.
3. Number the spaces in the empty egg carton 1 to 12.
4. Place one of the 11 symbols inside a plastic Easter egg. Then mold the clay around each egg, leaving the last egg empty.
5. Let the eggs air dry for 24 hours and then place them in the properly numbered space in the empty egg carton (you can also use a permanent marker to gently number the eggs as well).
6. Beginning 12 days before Easter, break open an egg each day revealing the object inside and the corresponding message.

CONCOCTION TIPS & IDEAS:

◆ In each egg, place an item along with a corresponding message and Scripture written on a small piece of paper (see list below).

◆ Each day discuss the enclosed object, and read the message and Scripture. Discuss it with your family. Leave the eggs open, showing its content. On the last day the egg is empty—just like Jesus' tomb!

◆ Make your eggs more festive by painting them with washable paint or decorating them with stickers.

◆ Make extra eggs with Scripture verses and other fun objects inside, perhaps a little toy, gift, or candy. Give these eggs to your friends and family members and share with them your love for Christ.

◆ This Easter story activity can help us remember the journey of Jesus in His final days on the earth and His ascent into heaven. This can be a great activity for the whole family to participate in or even become a family tradition.

EGG 1
Message: Jesus rode into Jerusalem on a donkey and people waved palm branches.
Passage: Matthew 21:1–11 / *Object:* A small plastic leaf or piece of a palm branch

EGG 2
Message: Mary poured perfume on Jesus' feet.
Passage: John 12:2–8 / *Object:* Small piece of cloth with perfume

EGG 3
Message: Jesus and His disciples ate the Last Supper.
Passage: Matthew 26:17–19 / *Object:* A crouton to represent the Passover bread

EGG 4
Message: Judas betrayed Jesus with 30 silver coins.
Passage: Matthew 27:3 / *Object:* A dime or "silver" coin

EGG 5
Message: Jesus carried the cross.
Passage: John 19:17 / *Object:* A small metal or plastic cross

EGG 6
Message: Soldiers placed a crown of thorns on Jesus' head.
Passage: John 19:2 / *Object:* A small thorny branch

EGG 7
Message: Soldiers cast lots for Jesus' garments.
Passage: John 19:23 / *Object:* Miniature dice

EGG 8
Message: Jesus was nailed to a cross.
Passage: John 19:18, 37 and John 20:25–29 / *Object:* Nail

EGG 9
Message: Jesus was given vinegar mixed with gall on sponge.
Passage: Matthew 27:48 / *Object:* A small piece of sponge

EGG 10
Message: Spices were used to prepare Jesus for burial.
Passage: John 19:40 / *Object:* Whole cloves

EGG 11
Message: The rock blocking Jesus' tomb was moved away.
Passage: John 20:1 / *Object:* A small rock

EGG 12
Message: Jesus has risen! The tomb is empty.
Passage: Luke 24:6 / *Object:* Nothing

HONEY LIP BALM

This tasty honey lip balm can be concocted in many delicious flavors. Just as honey tastes sweet in our mouths, the words God shares with us in the Bible are sweet to the heart and soul.

WHAT YOU WILL NEED:

2 Tbs. solid shortening (any flavor)

1 Tbs. or 1 envelope unsweetened powdered drink mix

1 tps. honey

1 plastic 35 mm-film container with lid (unused or well-washed)

HOW TO CONCOCT IT:

1. Place the shortening in a bowl and microwave on high for 30 seconds until the shortening is completely melted.

2. Have an adult remove the melted shortening from the microwave and stir in honey and drink mix.

3. Pour the mixture into the plastic film container. Do not pour into the container any sediment that has settled in the bowl. Place in the refrigerator for 30 to 45 minutes or until firm.

CONCOCTION TIPS & IDEAS:

◆ Decorate the film container using markers or stickers. You can also make a lip balm necklace by tying string or yarn around the plastic container and wearing it around your neck.

◆ It makes us feel good to taste something sweet. And it makes us feel good when we read in the Bible about how much God loves us, how we are each wonderfully made, and of God's loving promises to us.

How sweet are your words to my taste, sweeter than honey to my mouth!
(Psalm 119:103)

"NO WORRY" BIRD COOKIES

Birds will love these tasty treats, which remind us that just as God cares for all the birds in the world, He will provide for all who seek to know and love Him.

WHAT YOU WILL NEED:

1 cup softened unsalted butter
3 beaten eggs
3 1/2 cups flour
1 tsp. baking soda
Pinch of salt
Peanut butter
Mixed birdseed
Drinking glasses of different sizes
Drinking straw

HOW TO CONCOCT IT:

1. Stir flour, baking soda, and salt together in a large bowl. Then add butter and eggs. Mix until blended.
2. Roll dough out on a floured surface and cut different-size circular shapes using different-size drinking glasses.
3. Make a hole toward the top center of each cookie using a drinking straw. Bake at 350 degrees for 10 to 12 minutes.
4. When the Bird Cookies are cool, tie a ribbon or string through the hole.
5. Spread peanut butter on each side of the cookie. Then roll the cookie in birdseed. Hang your Bird Cookie from a tree, and watch the birds enjoy their tasty snack.

Look at the birds of the air; they do not sow or reap or store away in barns, and yet your heavenly Father feeds them. . . . Who of you by worrying can add a single hour to his life?
(Matthew 6:26–27)

CONCOCTION TIPS & IDEAS:

◆ You can make a classic bird feeder by rolling a pinecone or crispy piece of toast covered with peanut butter in birdseed and then hang from a tree using string or yarn.

◆ We should always remember when we see the birds flying in the sky how God takes care of them and always provides them whatever they need—food, shelter, and water. We should also trust in Him who provides so much for all of us.

EDIBLE OCEAN IN A BAG

This tasty treat looks like the goldfish-in-a-bag many of us have won at a church fair or carnival. Jesus spoke of us being fishers of men. He was saying that He wants us to go and share the good news of Christ with others.

WHAT YOU WILL NEED:

4 cups pre-made blueberry-flavored gelatin

4 clear plastic food or party favor bags

Gummy fish or Swedish fish

Ribbon

HOW TO CONCOCT IT:

1. Fill a clear plastic party favor bag with blueberry gelatin.
2. Gently push 1 or 2 orange Gummy/Swedish fish inside the gelatin.
3. You can add optional accessories like string licorice (for seaweed) and blueberries or grapes in the bottom (for rocks).
4. Tie the bag shut with a ribbon.

CONCOCTION TIPS & IDEAS:

◆ Fill a clear plastic party favor bag with blueberry gelatin and place an orange or red Gummy/Swedish fish inside and tie the bag shut with a ribbon. This will look like the goldfish-in-a-bag from the carnival or fair.

◆ It is pleasing to God when we give Him thanks and praise for all He does in our lives. Another way to please Him is to share His Word with others so they may know Him too.

"Come, follow me" Jesus said, "and I will make you fishers of men. (Matthew 4:19)

FRIENDSHIP STONE

True friendship is a wonderful gift from God. With the Friendship Stone project, you can create a unique symbol to celebrate friendship that will last for many years to come.

WHAT YOU WILL NEED:

Old bucket

8 cups quick-setting fine cement (nontoxic)

Water

Shallow cardboard box (11 x 16 works best) or disposable aluminum pans

Stick or large wooden spoon for stirring

Old ruler

Decorations for your stone

Stick or pencil for writing

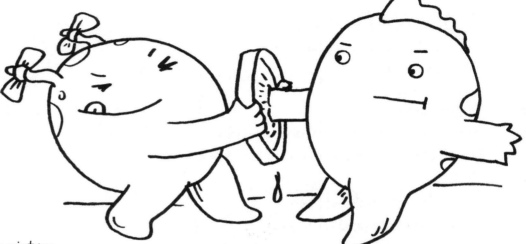

HOW TO CONCOCT IT:

1. Mix cement and 2 cups of water together in a bucket until the mixture is the consistency of oatmeal. Add more cement or water if necessary.

2. Pour the mixture evenly into the cardboard box or aluminum pan. Your cement layer should be about 2 inches thick. Then take an old ruler and smooth out the top of the cement. Wait 3 to 5 minutes.

3. Push your hand into the far right or left side of the wet cement. Push down at least 1 inch to make your impression. Have your friend place his or her hand in the wet cement and make an impression on the opposite side. Wash your hands immediately.

4. Use a stick or pencil to write your names, date, and a favorite Scripture.

CONCOCTION TIPS & IDEAS:

◆ While the cement is still wet, personalize your Friendship Stone by adding items that mean something to both of you—seashells, coins, plastic toys, old jewelry, marbles, etc.

◆ Time and weather can change the face of a rock, yet the rock remains strong at its core. A good friendship is like that—colored and shaped by time and circumstances but solid and dependable at its core.

There is a friend who sticks closer than a brother.
(Proverbs 18:24)

HYDRO JET ARK

One of the favorite Bible stories for children is the story of Noah. God instructed Noah to build an ark to save his family and two of every animal from a flood that would cover the entire planet. In honor of Noah's story, this is a floating vessel that zips across the water!

WHAT YOU WILL NEED:

1 plastic 16 oz. soda bottle with cap

1/4 cup vinegar

1 Tbs. baking soda

Plastic straw

White glue (do not use washable glue) or low-temp glue gun

Plastic stickers (paper-based stickers will wash off)

HOW TO CONCOCT IT:

1. Ask an adult to poke a hole in the lower side of the plastic bottle.
2. Insert a straw into the hole, leaving 1 inch hanging out.
3. Seal the air cracks around the straw with glue. Let the glue completely dry before continuing.
4. Pour vinegar into the bottle. Add baking soda and quickly put the cap back on the plastic bottle.
5. Place the Hydro Jet Ark into a tub of water and watch it go!

CONCOCTION TIPS & IDEAS:

◆ Make 2 or more arks and have a race to see whose ark can go farther.

◆ God protected Noah by giving him shelter in the ark. God then promised that He would never flood the whole earth again. God loves and protects each of us every day of our lives.

Noah did everything just as God commanded him.
(Genesis 6:22)

1 tbls. baking soda

¼ c. of Vinegar

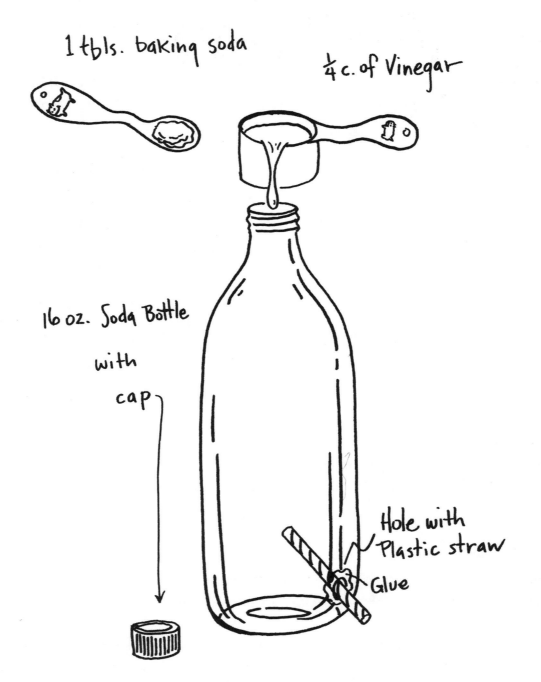

16 oz. Soda Bottle

with

cap

Hole with
Plastic straw

Glue

LIVING BASKET

This basket is a wonderful way to bring the beauty of outdoors inside and is an alternative to plastic Easter basket grass. Use this project to illustrate the parable of the sower of seeds told by Jesus in Matthew 13.

WHAT YOU WILL NEED:

Colored plastic wrap

Grass seed (wheat seed or rye seed)

Potting soil

Basket

Plant mister

HOW TO CONCOCT IT:

1. Line the basket with plastic wrap, leaving 1 inch hanging over the basket.
2. Fill the basket with 4 or more inches of clean potting soil.
3. Sprinkle a thin layer of grass seed over the soil and cover the seed with 1/4 inch of potting soil. Then water the seeds with the plant mister.
4. Place the basket in a warm, sunny window. Spray the soil with a plant mister 2 or 3 times a day. Make sure the soil is always moist. Be careful not to overwater or underwater the grass seed.
5. After 4 or 5 days, the grass will begin to sprout. You should have a beautiful basket of grass in 2 to 3 weeks.

CONCOCTION TIPS & IDEAS:

◆ Decorate the basket with ribbons and accessories, or use a small toy house, stones, and twigs to create an ornamental garden any time of the year. You can also add colored eggs or spring flowers for Easter.

◆ We want to be a sower of good seeds in the good soil of our own lives. If we place ourselves (the seed) in the hands of Jesus (the good soil), then we will grow into something beautiful, because we grow in the things of Christ.

Still other seed fell on good soil, where it produced a crop—a hundred, sixty or thirty times what was sown.
(Matthew 13:8)

COLOR-CHANGE BATH SALTS

These bath salts will change your bath time into a colorful and relaxing event. We can also find rest for our soul as we think about the Lord during our quiet bath time.

WHAT YOU WILL NEED:

1 clear plastic peanut butter jar (clean with the label removed)

2 cups Epsom salt

1 cup coarse sea salt

Food coloring

Perfume

4 pint-size plastic ziplock bags

HOW TO CONCOCT IT:

1. Mix both kinds of salt together in a bowl. Add 5 to 6 drops of perfume and stir.

2. Divide the salt equally into 4 different plastic ziplock bags. Add 2 to 3 drops of food coloring to each bag. Be sure to use a different color for each bag.

3. Seal each bag and shake until the salt is a solid, even color.

4. Spoon the salt mixture into the jar, creating different-colored layers. Continue until the jar is full; then screw on the lid.

CONCOCTION TIPS & IDEAS:

◆ Decorate the jar by placing a small square of fabric over the lid, securing it with a rubber band. Make a label with the name of the fragrance and directions for use "Add 1/3 to 1/2 cup of Color-Change Bath Salts to a full tub of warm water."

◆ Try creating these relaxing bath salts as a gift for someone you care about. Use a ribbon and attach a gift tag to the jar. Write on it the Scripture to the right to encourage the recipient to find their rest in the Lord. A fun and relaxing bath will help them to remember that the Lord can give rest in our hearts when we are feeling tired and worn out. One of the ways we can find this rest is by spending quiet time with Him in prayer.

"Come to me, all you who are weary and burdened, and I will give you rest." (Matthew 11:28)

SPARKLING GLITTER CANDLES

These bright, festive candles symbolize how God takes those who obey His Word and raises them out of the darkness and into the light. He will always help us to find our way, no matter how dark our circumstances.

WHAT YOU WILL NEED:

Pillar candle

White glue

Paintbrush

Gold glitter

HOW TO CONCOCT IT:

1. Paint the sides of the candle with a thin layer of white glue.
2. Sprinkle the sides of the candle with glitter.
3. Let the candle dry overnight before handling.

CONCOCTION TIPS & IDEAS:

◆ Decorate several pillar candles of various sizes using the same or different colors of glitter. Place the candles on a gold or silver plate to create a beautiful centerpiece for any occasion.

◆ Just as light from a candle helps us see where to go and turns a dark room into one filled with light, our way becomes clearer as God enters into our situation. The paths we take in life and the choices we make become clearer as we know Him more and learn to live in ways pleasing to Him.

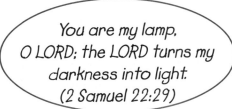

You are my lamp,
O LORD; the LORD turns my
darkness into light.
(2 Samuel 22:29)

FLOWER TRANSFERS

This project allows you to capture and preserve the God-given beauty of a flower for years to come. You can create wonderful pieces of art with natural fresh flowers.

WHAT YOU WILL NEED:

Rubber mallet or hammer
Plastic wrap
Fresh flowers (pansies, impatiens, and geraniums work best)
Paper

HOW TO CONCOCT IT:

1. Arrange the flowers face down on a sheet of paper.
2. Carefully cover the flowers with a clear sheet of plastic wrap.
3. Gently hit the flowers with the rubber mallet or hammer, being careful not to miss any parts of the flower.
4. Remove the plastic wrap and the flowers from the paper to reveal your work of art.

CONCOCTION TIPS & IDEAS:

◆ Use Flower Transfers to create stationery sets, greeting cards, and wrapping paper. You can also use the flower-transfer technique on 100 percent cotton T-shirts, napkins, and placemats.

◆ God made flowers so perfect and so beautiful, then decorated our world with them. Using flowers to decorate our homes or making these works of art reminds us of this beautiful gift He gave us to enjoy.

As for man, his days are like grass, he flourishes like a flower of the field.
(Psalm 103:15)

LIVING WORDS

You can plant and care for seeds that will grow into living, inspirational words. This is a fun way to learn the responsibility of planting and caring for the seeds God made for us.

WHAT YOU WILL NEED:

Grass seed (choose a fast-growing type of seed)

Potting soil

3- to 4-inch deep dish

Pencil or stick

Plant mister

HOW TO CONCOCT IT:

1. Fill the dish with 2 to 3 inches of potting soil.

2. Moisten the soil with a plant mister.

3. Use a pencil or stick to write words or draw a simple
   picture in the soil. This will create little trenches to plant the seeds in.

4. Carefully sprinkle seeds into the trenches you've made.

5. Gently cover the seeds with a thin layer of soil and water with the plant mister. Place your dish where it will get plenty of sunlight.

6. Use the plant mister to lightly moisten the soil 2 to 3 times a day. Your words or picture will begin to sprout in 7 to 10 days.

CONCOCTION TIPS & IDEAS:

◆ Try using chive seeds instead of grass seeds.

◆ If the grass grows too long, your words or picture may become illegible. If this happens. trim
   the grass with scissors.

◆ You can write words to inspire you—faith, hope, love, trust, dream. Or you can draw symbols like a heart, a smile, or a cross.

◆ In 1 Corinthians 3:6, the seeds Paul is speaking of planting are seeds of hope. Paul said that Apollos watered the seeds because
   Apollos shared more about Jesus with others. These men planted and watered the seeds,
   but God made them grow.

> *I planted the seed,
> Apollos watered it, but God
> made it grow.
> (1 Corinthians 3:6)*

CREATION SAND PLAQUES

Creation Sand Plaques are pieces of art that honor God and celebrate His creations. This project reminds us to give thanks for all of the wonderful things He has made.

WHAT YOU WILL NEED:

2 cups quick-setting plaster of Paris
1 cup water
Sand
Paper clip
Pan or large bowl

HOW TO CONCOCT IT:

1. Fill the pan or bowl with sand. Lightly sprinkle the sand with water until the sand is moist enough to hold an impression.
2. Make an impression in the sand using a solid natural object like a seashell, small twig, rock, or your own handprint.
3. Immediately pour the plaster mixture into the sand impression. Be careful not to let the plaster touch the edge of the pan or the plaque will be hard to remove.
4. Slightly pull apart the paper clip; then push one end of the paper clip into the wet plaster to make a hanger for the plaque.

CONCOCTION TIPS & IDEAS:

◆ Create color-tinted plaques by stirring kids' paint or food coloring into the plaster mixture immediately after you add the water.
◆ Scripture tells us that He created the world we live in and everything in it. Most importantly, God reminds us that He does not live just in temples or churches; He lives everywhere.

> The God who made the world and everything in it is the Lord of heaven and earth.
> (Acts 17:24)

SPLONGEE BALL OF VIRTUES

This soft starburst-shaped ball is fun to play with indoors and out. It becomes a fun and easy way to remember the virtues and character traits God wants us to have as His children.

WHAT YOU WILL NEED:

3 large nylon square sponges
1 plastic cable tie
Scissors

HOW TO CONCOCT IT:

1. Cut each sponge in half lengthwise.
2. Stack the cut sponges on top of each other in three rows of two. As you put them together, give each of the strips a name of one of the virtues from our Scripture verse below.
3. Grab the stack of sponges in the center and twist the stack once.
4. Secure a plastic cable tie around the center of the twisted stack, pulling it as tight as possible. This represents the love that binds together these virtues.
5. Trim the plastic cable tie down as close to the eye as possible.

CONCOCTION TIPS & IDEAS:

◆ Wet your Splongee Ball and take it outside for a game of "splash ball." You can also play soccer or vollleyball with your Splongee Ball.
◆ Memorize the six virtues we assigned to the sponge strips. Stand with a friend or in a group. Name the six virtues God tells us to have in the book of Colossians, remembering that the cable tie that binds the ball together represents love. If one person recites the virtues correctly, toss them the ball and let someone else have a turn.

> Therefore,
> as God's chosen people, . . .
> clothe yourselves with compassion,
> kindness, humility, gentleness, and patience.
> Bear with each other and forgive whatever griev-
> ances you may have against one another. Forgive
> as the Lord forgave you. And over all these
> virtues put on love.
> (Colossians 3:12–14)

HEAVENLY TREASURES BOTTLE

Children will have fun searching for hidden treasures while learning about the Bible. God's Word tells us that the treasures of this earth—money, gold, silver, and other material things—are not nearly as important as the treasures God wants us to possess.

WHAT YOU WILL NEED:

1 clear plastic 16 oz. soda bottle with cap (clean with label removed)
Light corn syrup
Assorted shapes of nonmetalic confetti (found in party supply
    stores and greeting-card shops)
Water
Assorted small, plastic objects that symbolize the teachings of the Bible.
    Ex: a dove, symbolizing peace; a cross, for Jesus' sacrifice and our
    salvation; a heart, showing God's love for us; fruits, to help us
    remember the fruits of the Spirit; a rock, for Jesus is the rock of
    our salvation; a star, to remember Jesus' birth; a fish, which
    symbolizes Jesus, the Son of God.

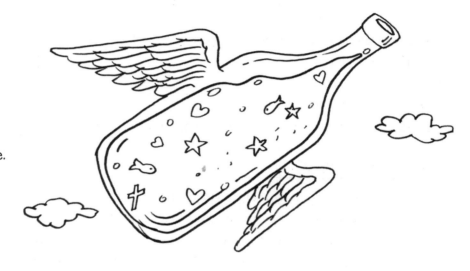

HOW TO CONCOCT IT:

1. Fill the soda bottle 3/4 full with corn syrup.
2. Add a small handful of confetti and the plastic objects. Then top the bottle off with water.
3. Seal the bottle securely with a cap and shake until clear.

CONCOCTION TIPS & IDEAS:

"Store up for yourselves treasures in heaven, where moth and rust do not destroy, and where thieves do not break in and steal." (Matthew 6:20)

◆ Make a list of the objects placed in the bottle and their meaning. Play a game by setting
    a 30-second time limit and then try to locate as many objects hidden in the bottle as possible before time runs out.
◆ The heavenly treasures God speaks of are eternal and will follow us forever, unlike the earthly treasures that are ultimately left behind.
    These godly treasures are found by praising, honoring, and obeying God and His commandments.

DIVINE DRYER LINT CLAY

Make art pieces like vases, decorative jars, and flower pots out of something we all throw in the trash—dryer lint! God can take things of little beauty and value and make them into something beautiful and priceless.

WHAT YOU WILL NEED:

3 cups dryer lint (new bright-colored sweatshirts make
    the best lint)
2 cups warm water
2/3 cup wheat flour
Decorative pieces such as plastic jewels, buttons, tiles, etc.

HOW TO CONCOCT IT:

1. Mix all ingredients together in a large pot.
2. Have an adult cook the mixture over low heat, stirring
    constantly until the mixture starts to hold together. Turn the
    heat off and let the mixture completely cool before handling.
3. Use Divine Dryer Lint Clay just as you would papier-mâché, forming
    it around bottles, vases, flower pots, bowls, and more.

CONCOCTION TIPS & IDEAS:

◆ Push plastic jewels, buttons, and small tiles into the wet clay to create your materpieces. Mold the clay around jars for flower vases,
    glass jar candles, and flower pots.
◆ By taking something we would throw away as trash and turning it into a work of art, we learn how God can make anything He
    chooses beautiful. God can show us beauty in many things.

He has made everything beautiful in its time. (Ecclesiastes 3:11)

WATER BALLOON YO-YO

This new version of a classic toy always bounces back, showing us how God lets us stumble and struggle sometimes in our lives, but He keeps us from falling completely and returns us safely to His hands.

WHAT YOU WILL NEED:

1 9-inch balloon
1 file-folder size rubber band

HOW TO CONCOCT IT:

1. Cut the rubber band in half.
2. Tie a secure loop on one end of the rubber band, large enough to slip around your finger.
3. Use a water faucet to fill the balloon 1/4 full of water.
4. Have an adult blow air into the balloon until it is approximately the size of a baseball. Then tie the balloon shut.
5. Securely tie the rubber band around the knot on the balloon.
6. Place the rubber band loop around your middle finger and gently throw the balloon toward the ground. When the balloon springs back toward your hand, try to grab it.

CONCOCTION TIPS & IDEAS:

◆ Use colored markers to decorate your Water Balloon Yo-Yo for holidays such as Easter and Christmas.
◆ Just like the yo-yo, our lives can bounce back into God's hands, even when we think we are going to fall helplessly to the ground. If we love and respect and walk with Him in every part of our lives, He will be faithful to protect us.

If the LORD delights in a man's way, he makes his steps firm; though he stumble, he will not fall, for the LORD upholds him with his hand.
(Psalm 37:23–24)

WORLD'S BEST BUBBLES

It's fun to create your own bubbles. We have tested dozens of bubble recipes and found this one to be the best of the best. You can use these bubbles to offer up praise to God in a fun and playful way.

WHAT YOU WILL NEED:

2 1/2 qts. water
1/2 cup light corn syrup
1 cup liquid dish detergent

HOW TO CONCOCT IT:

1. Mix the water and corn syrup together until completely blended.
2. Gently stir in the liquid dish detergent.
3. World's Best Bubbles will store for several weeks in an airtight container.

CONCOCTION TIPS & IDEAS:

◆ Add a little color to your bubbles by stirring in a few drops of food coloring. Dip a bubble wand, plastic strawberry basket, or wire whisk into the solutions to blow the bubbles.
◆ The Bible tells us that everything that has breath should praise the Lord. As you use your breath to send bubbles high into the sky, think of praising the Lord. Offer Him praise for He is good.

Let everything that has breath praise the LORD. Praise the LORD. (Psalm 150:6)

BUBBLE PAINT

Use this concoction to create bright, colorful bubble paints. Create a keepsake photo frame to showcase a picture of a family member, friend, or pet as a way to give thanks to God for your loved ones.

WHAT YOU WILL NEED:

2 tsp. clear liquid dish detergent

1/4 cup water

2 to 3 Tbs. kids' paint or washable poster paint

Photo mat

HOW TO CONCOCT IT:

1. Mix the dish detergent, water, and paint together in a small, shallow bowl. If you are using concentrated dish detergent, you may need to add 1 to 2 more tablespoons of water.
2. Using a straw, gently blow into the paint mixture until a dome of bubbles form. (DO NOT DRINK IT!)
3. Capture bubble prints by placing the photo mat or paper on top of the bubble dome.
4. Repeat the process, using different colors of bubble paint.

CONCOCTION TIPS & IDEAS:

◆ Use Bubble Paint to create custom stationery, envelopes, greeting cards, wrapping paper, invitations, and cool gift bags.
◆ Make a frame for a gift for someone you love and write the Scripture verse below on the border of the frame.

I thank my God every time
I remember you.
(Philippians 1:3)

SCRIPTURE SIDEWALK CHALK

With this concoction you can create any size, color, and shape of Scripture Sidewalk Chalk imaginable. Kids can use the chalk to create images of themselves on the sidewalk to celebrate how God made each of us special.

WHAT YOU WILL NEED:

1/3 cup quick-setting plaster of Paris (nontoxic)

2 Tbs. kids' paint or washable poster paint

3 Tbs. water

Candy mold, soap mold, plastic ice cube tray, or toilet paper
   tube (taped shut on one end)

HOW TO CONCOCT IT:

1. Mix plaster, paint, and water together in a small bowl.
2. Quickly spoon the mixture into a candy mold, soap mold, plastic ice tray, or toilet paper tube taped shut on one end.
3. Let the chalk dry for an hour or until completely solid.
4. Carefully remove the chalk from the mold.

CONCOCTION TIPS & IDEAS:

◆ Create rainbow chalk by layering different colors of wet plaster. You can also add glitter to create sparkling chalk.

◆ Have someone trace your body as you lay on the cement. Write your name by your figure outline and decorate yourself with eyes, ears, mouth, and even clothes. Take turns with family and friends laying side by side and draw everyone holding hands. Write below your drawings; "I am fearfully and wonderfully made."

*I praise you because I am fearfully and wonderfully made; your works are wonderful, I know that full well.
(Psalm 139:14)*

SUPER SIDEWALK PAINT

Now you can color large portions of sidewalk space in just a fraction of the time it would take with traditional stick chalk. Celebrate all the things God created by making murals on your sidewalk. You can also make drawings inspired by the stories in the Bible.

WHAT YOU WILL NEED:

1/4 cup cornstarch
1/4 cold water
Food coloring

HOW TO CONCOCT IT:

1. Mix cornstarch and water together in a small bowl.
2. Add 6 to 8 drops of food coloring and stir.
3. Repeat this process to create different colors of sidewalk paint.

CONCOCTION TIPS & IDEAS:

◆ Use at church fairs or picnics to set up fun games like cakewalks and hopscotch and to write inspirational messages.
◆ Draw and paint scenes of the things from God's world you love and enjoy. Maybe it's the sun, clouds, and green grass. Maybe it's animals or people you love. Or you can make murals of Bible stores like Noah's ark, Jonah and the whale, or David and Goliath. It helps us remember all the great deeds God has done in our lives and in the lives of those who lived before us.

May your deeds be shown to your servants, your splendor to their children. (Psalm 90:16)

DAVID'S SLINGSHOT FLYER

This soft slingshot flyer is fun to play with indoors or out. It reminds us that God's Word will always prevail. We can be triumphant in our lives with God's help and instruction, just as David was.

WHAT YOU WILL NEED:

3 small nylon kitchen sponges (3 different colors, if possible)

1 plastic cable tie

1 file-folder rubber band

Scissors

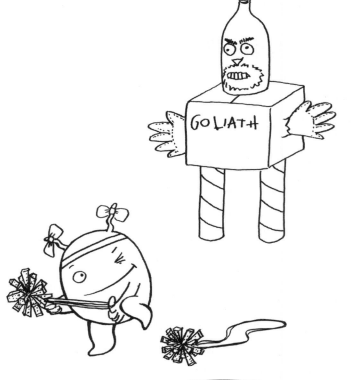

HOW TO CONCOCT IT:

1. Cut each sponge into thirds lengthwise.
2. Stack the cut sponges on top of each other in three rows of three.
3. Grab the stack of sponges in the center and twist the stack once.
4. Place the plastic cable tie through the center of the rubber band.
5. Secure the plastic cable tie around the center of the twisted stack, pulling it as tightly as possible.
6. Trim the plastic cable tie as close to the eye as possible.
7. Put the rubber band on the tip of your thumb, pull back the flyer, and release.

CONCOCTION TIPS & IDEAS:

◆ Play a game of David and Goliath by decorating several empty plastic bottles, shoot the flyer, and try to knock over the bottles..

◆ Read and discuss the story of David and Goliath from the Bible or storybook. Discuss how David was triumphant in his battle by calling on the power of God and His word. It is a story of great faith in which a mere boy, with only a slingshot and some stones from the stream, defeated a nine-foot-tall giant in full battle armor and armed with a mighty sword and spear..

David said to the Philistine, "You come against me with sword and spear and javelin, but I come against you in the name of the LORD Almighty, the God of the armies of Israel. (1 Samuel 17:45)

MOSES' MIRACLE MUCK

Just as God parted the Red Sea long enough for Moses and the Israelites to cross to the other side, Miracle Muck transforms from a liquid to a solid and back to liquid again. This project reminds us of one of the many miracles God has performed to save His people and show His power.

WHAT YOU WILL NEED:

3/4 cup cornstarch
1/3 cup water
Blue food coloring

HOW TO CONCOCT IT:

1. Mix water and 5 to 7 drops of food coloring together in a small bowl.
2. Slowly add cornstarch to the mixture. (DO NOT STIR!)
3. Let the mixture stand for 2 to 3 minutes.
4. Pick up a handful of Moses' Miracle Muck and squeeze it until it forms a hard ball. As you hold the ball in your hand, it will amazingly turn back into a liquid again!

CONCOCTION TIPS & IDEAS:

◆ Experiment by adding different proportions of water and cornstarch.
◆ With God anything is possible. Moses and the Israelites were about to be destroyed as they were trapped at the edge of the sea. God parted the sea, creating walls out of water. Moses led God's people through the sea on dry ground. Then God closed the sea again as their enemies pursued them. God saves His people in their time of need.

Then Moses stretched out his hand over the sea. . . . The waters were divided, and the Israelites went through the sea on dry ground, with a wall of water on their right and on their left.
(Exodus 14:21-22)

CINNAMON HEART ORNAMENTS

These heart-shaped ornaments are not only fun to make, but they smell great too! It is a tradition in our family to make these ornaments each Christmas season. Family traditions create heartwarming memories and strengthen the family bond.

WHAT YOU WILL NEED:

1/2 cup cinnamon
1/2 cup applesauce
Plastic ziplock bag
Heart-shaped cookie cutter
Drinking straw
Ribbon or string
Gift tags

HOW TO CONCOCT IT:

1. Pour the cinnamon and applesauce into the plastic ziplock bag.
2. Seal the bag and knead until the mixture turns to dough.
3. Lightly dust a hard surface with cinnamon and roll out the dough. Then use a heart-shaped cookie cutter and cut out your ornament.
4. Before the dough dries, use a drinking straw to make a small hole about 1/4 inch from the top of your cutout so it can be hung with ribbon or string.
5. Let your Cinnamon Heart Ornaments air dry in a warm place for 1 to 2 days or until hard. Flip the ornaments over several times each day to make sure both sides dry.
6. Write the Scripture listed on the right on a gift tag and attach to the ornament.

Teach me your way, O LORD, and I will walk in your truth; give me an undivided heart, that I may fear your name. (Psalm 86:11)

CONCOCTION TIPS & IDEAS:

◆ Use cookie cutters of different shapes, along with the other Scriptures, to add more of God's Word to our holiday tree.
◆ Let your ornaments remind you to pray that God will help you always have a pure heart full of love for Him and the wisdom to walk in His ways.

WASHABLE WINDOW ART

Use this washable paint to create awesome works of art on windows. Decorate your windows with hearts, angels, a cross, or a rainbow to profess your faith and celebrate the holidays. This is a great way to declare that your home is a house of the Lord.

WHAT YOU WILL NEED:

2 Tbs. clear liquid dish detergent
1 Tbs. washable poster paint or liquid tempera paint
Paintbrushes

HOW TO CONCOCT IT:

1. Mix liquid dish detergent and paint together in a small bowl.
2. Repeat the above step using several different colors of paint.
3. Dip your brush into the window paint and paint on a glass window or glass door. Be careful not to get paint on woodwork, caulking, or other nonglass surfaces.

CONCOCTION TIPS & IDEAS:

◆ Remove Washable Window Art with paper towels and glass cleaner.
◆ Profess your faith in God and the faith of your whole household by creating these fun works of arts on the windows or doors of your home. When your neighbors ask about the decorations, tell them about Jesus and how God loves them too.

As for me and my household, we will serve the LORD.
(Joshua 24:15)

JIGGLE ORANGE SLICES

These tasty treats look just like real orange wedges and make a perfect low-fat snack. God provides us with so much in our lives, and these tasty, creative treats remind us that all good things come from God.

WHAT YOU WILL NEED:

Oranges
1 box of orange-flavored gelatin

HOW TO CONCOCT IT:

1. Have an adult cut the oranges in half and scoop out the center leaving the outer skin.
2. Prepare the box of orange gelatin following the printed instructions on the package.
3. Pour the warm liquid gelatin into each of the orange halves.
4. Place the orange halves in the refrigerator to gel for 8 hours.
5. Remove the oranges from the refrigerator and have an adult cut the oranges into wedges.

CONCOCTION TIPS & IDEAS:

◆ Use different types of citrus fruit—grapefruit, lemon, lime—along with different flavors of gelatin to create unique treats.
◆ These fun fruits celebrate the sweet fruits God provides for us. He loves us so much that He gives us not only foods to help us grow, but also gives us ones that taste sweet and good to our lips.

If you follow my decrees and are careful to obey my commands, I will send you rain in its season, and the ground will yield its crops and the trees of the field their fruit.
(Leviticus 26:3-4)

SUPER BUBBLE SLIME

This amazing concoction creates slimy, stretchy putty that transforms into a bouncing ball and even blows up like a balloon! We can only imagine being caught in a large pit of slime and unable to get out. God tells us that He can rescue us from the pits and struggles of our lives and bring us out safely.

WHAT YOU WILL NEED:

1/4 cup liquid laundry starch
1/4 cup school glue gel
1 drop food coloring
Plastic ziplock bag or airtight container

HOW TO CONCOCT IT:

1. Pour school glue gel into a small bowl. Add 1 drop of food coloring and stir until blended.
2. Slowly pour the mixture into a bowl containing the liquid starch.
3. Let the mixture sit for 5 minutes. Remove it from the bowl, then slowly knead it with your hands until the glue absorbs almost all of the liquid starch. The more you knead your Super Bubble Slime, the firmer it will become.
4. Store Super Bubble Slime in a plastic ziplock bag or airtight container.

CONCOCTION TIPS & IDEAS:

◆ Wrap a blob of the Bubble Slime on the end of a straw and blow a large bubble.
◆ Although slime can be fun to play with, none of us wants to live in a pit of slime, mud, and muck. The Bible reminds us that God is faithful to rescue us from this type of pit and to give us a new direction in our lives and a new song in our heart. Life can be a terribly lonely place, impossible to escape without Him.

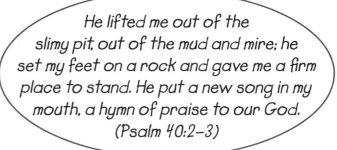

He lifted me out of the slimy pit, out of the mud and mire; he set my feet on a rock and gave me a firm place to stand. He put a new song in my mouth, a hymn of praise to our God. (Psalm 40:2–3)

TEN COMMANDMENTS PAINT PENS

These no-drip, roll-on paint pens never dry out. You can use them to draw pictures representing some of the commandments God gave to Moses and his people.

WHAT YOU WILL NEED:

Empty roll-on deodorant bottles
Liquid tempera paint or washable poster paint
Paper

HOW TO CONCOCT IT:

1. Have an adult carefully remove the roll-on ball from the deodorant bottle.
2. Rinse the bottle with water. Then fill it with paint and snap the roll-on ball back into the bottle.
3. Shake the container and begin rolling to get the paint started.
4. Paint by rolling the ball across the paper.

CONCOCTION TIPS & IDEAS:

◆ Make several paint pens with different colors of paint. Make a label on the outside to identify each color.
◆ Paint pens are great for young children and are easy to clean up after.
◆ God gave Moses the commandments when Moses was alone spending quiet time with Him. God can give us wisdom and share things with us during our quiet prayer time too. It is important that we give God time and listen so that He can speak to our hearts.

> Then the LORD said to Moses, "Write down these words, . . . I have made a covenant with you and with Israel." Moses . . . wrote on the tablets the words of the covenant—the Ten Commandments. (Exodus 34:27–28)

THE TEN COMMANDMENTS

1. PUT GOD FIRST
2. WORSHIP GOD ONLY
3. USE GOD'S NAME WITH RESPECT
4. REMEMBER THE SABBATH
5. RESPECT YOUR PARENTS
6. DO NOT HURT OTHERS
7. BE FAITHFUL IN MARRIAGE
8. DO NOT STEAL
9. DO NOT LIE
10. DO NOT ENVY OTHERS' LIVES OR POSSESSIONS

SHOWER TIME PAINTS

Have fun painting while getting yourself and the shower or tub clean at the same time! Just like soap washes the dirt away from our bodies, God can wash our hearts and our souls clean from sin by His forgiveness.

WHAT YOU WILL NEED:

1/4 cup baby bath or baby shampoo
1 Tbs. cornstarch
Food coloring or washable liquid colorant
Plastic ice cube trays or small plastic cups

HOW TO CONCOCT IT:

1. Mix baby bath or shampoo with cornstarch in a small bowl.
2. Pour the mixture, in equal parts, into several sections of a plastic ice cube tray or plastic cups.
3. Add 1 to 2 drops washable liquid colorant or food coloring to each section of the tray and stir.
4. Use on the side of the bathtub or shower. Do not use on tile or grout.

CONCOCTION TIPS & IDEAS:

◆ Use Shower Time Paints with a paintbrush or your fingers.
◆ We should always have a heart full of praise and thanks. Even when we do bad things or think bad thoughts, God still loves us. He is always ready to forgive us when we ask Him. Using your Shower Time Paints, draw some other things that you are thankful to God for giving you—maybe your family, pet, home, clothes, food, friends, a special trip or vacation, or a special gift.

Wash away all my iniquity and cleanse me from my sin.
(Psalm 51:2)

BEAUTIFUL-IN-TIME MARBLEIZING

Create beautiful marbleized paper in a rainbow of colors. You will be surprised how a messy plate of shaving cream can be used to make beautiful pieces of stationery, greeting cards, and gift wrap. God makes everything beautiful in its proper time.

WHAT YOU WILL NEED:

Foamy shaving cream (nongel)
Paper plate
Toothpick
Food coloring
Paper towels
Paper

HOW TO CONCOCT IT:

1. Cover the paper plate with a 1-inch layer of shaving cream.
2. Smooth out the shaving cream with a spatula so it is flat and smooth.
3. Add several randomly placed drops of food coloring on top of the shaving cream. Using 3 different colors works best.
4. Using a toothpick, gently swirl the food coloring into the shaving cream. Be careful not to swirl the colors too much, or they will turn dark and start to look muddy.
5. Place a sheet of paper on top of the shaving cream and gently push down on the paper. Remove the paper from the shaving cream and wipe off the shaving cream using a paper towel.

CONCOCTION TIPS & IDEAS:

◆ Just as the messy plate of shaving cream produces something of beauty, so it is with our lives. We can't always see the beauty or purpose in ourselves or in the situations God allows us to go through in this life. We will not fully understand God's purpose for our lives while we are on earth. But as we mature in our faith, God will begin to show us how awkward or troubling times have made us more like Christ.

Put on the new self, created to be like God in true righteousness and holiness. (Ephesians 4:24)

HOLIDAY PEPPERMINT WREATHS

Peppermint wreaths are a great alternative to hanging candy canes on the Christmas tree and also make wonderful gifts and package ties.

WHAT YOU WILL NEED:

Bag of round peppermint discs
Tin foil
Cookie sheet
Ribbon

HOW TO CONCOCT IT:

1. Cover the cookie sheet with tin foil.
2. Arrange several peppermint discs in a circle on the covered cookie sheet, making sure the discs are touching each other.
3. Place the cookie sheet in a preheated oven at 250 degrees for 3 to 5 minutes or until the peppermint discs start to melt together.
4. Have an adult remove the cookie sheet from the oven; then use the back of a spoon to gently press the warm candy together. Let the Peppermint Wreaths cool for 10 minutes. Use a spatula to carefully remove the cooled Peppermint Wreaths from the foil.

CONCOCTION TIPS & IDEAS:

◆ Use different types of hard candy and your imagination to create wreaths and other designs like a cross or heart-shaped wreath. Tie a ribbon around your wreaths and use them as ornaments or gifts.
◆ These candy wreaths remind us that God can take our sins, represented by the scarlet red, and make them white as snow, if we will be obedient to Him. He also tells us that He will give us the best to eat from the land. Remember this as you enjoy these tasty treats!

"Though your sins are like scarlet, they shall be as white as snow; though they are red as crimson, they shall be like wool. If you are willing and obedient, you will eat the best from the land."
(Isaiah 1:18–19)

SHAKE-AND-MAKE SLUSHY

Make a delicious slushy in just minutes using fruit juice, soda, or your favorite sports drink. Just as the cool slushy refreshes us on a warm day, we can refresh others by living a life that pleases God.

WHAT YOU WILL NEED:

1 gallon-size plastic ziplock bag
6 Tbs. rock salt or kosher salt (pretzel salt)
1 pint-size plastic ziplock bag
Ice (enough to fill half of the gallon-size ziplock bag)
1 cup juice, soda, fruit punch, or sports drink

HOW TO CONCOCT IT:

1. Fill the gallon-size plastic bag half full with ice and add
2. Pour the juice, soda, fruit punch, or sports drinks into pint-size ziplock bag and seal.
3. Place the pint-size bag inside the gallon-size bag. Seal the gallon-size bag.
4. Shake the bag for 5 to 7 minutes. Open the small bag and enjoy!

CONCOCTION TIPS & IDEAS:

◆ Create lemon ice simply by using lemonade in your slushy mix.
◆ Just like our slushy is refreshing and tastes cool as snow, the Bible tells us that delivering the good news of God's love refreshes the hearts of others. Scripture also tells us that being a trustworthy and dependable messenger will make God happy.

Like the coolness of snow at harvest time is a trustworthy messenger of those who send him.
(Proverbs 25:13)

SURPRISE SOAPS

Ball-shaped soaps reveal secret treasures inside as children wash. As you wash with your Surprise Soap to see what is inside, spend time in prayer asking God to show you what you have hidden inside that you need to confess to Him. He can wash away your sins and make you clean.

WHAT YOU WILL NEED:

1 cup grated Ivory soap
1/4 cup warm water
Food coloring
Small plastic or rubber toys

HOW TO CONCOCT IT:

1. Mix water, grated soap, and a few drops of food coloring together in a medium bowl. Stir the mixture until it begins to stiffen.
2. Remove the mixture from the bowl and knead it until it is the consistency of very thick dough.
3. Roll the dough into the shape of a ball.
4. Make a hole in the center of the ball large enough to hide treasures in.
5. Fill the hole with a treasure and seal the hole with some extra dough.
6. Allow Surprise Soaps to dry overnight before using.

Cleanse me . . . and I will be clean; wash me, and I will be whiter than snow. (Psalm 51:7)

CONCOCTION TIPS & IDEAS:

◆ Mold the soap dough into different shapes and sizes, or roll it out and cut with a cookie cutter.
◆ Bath time can be a great place for quiet time with God. God's Word tells us we are cleansed when He forgives us and takes the sin from us. No soap can ever clean the inside of our soul and our hearts like God can. When we have done wrong, we should confess it to Him in prayer, ask forgiveness, and with a pure heart tell Him we will learn from our mistakes and not do it again.

SPAGHETTI ICE CREAM SUNDAE

Don't be fooled. This project looks like a sauce-covered plate of spaghetti, but it is actually a delicious ice cream sundae! Ice cream is one of the favorite desires of children everywhere. God tells us when we delight in Him and obey Him, He will give us the desires of our heart.

WHAT YOU WILL NEED:

Vanilla ice cream (softened)

Cookie press or pasta maker

Strawberry topping

HOW TO CONCOCT IT:

1. Place softened vanilla ice cream in a cookie press or pasta maker. Use a die that will produce long, spaghetti-like strings.
2. Squeeze the ice cream strings onto a plate.
3. Top with strawberry topping and enjoy!

CONCOCTION TIPS & IDEAS:

◆ Use different flavors of ice cream and toppings to create a Spaghetti Ice Cream Sundae bar.

◆ When we seek Him and obey His Word, God loves to bless us with things our hearts delight in—just as our parents like to bless us when we are obedient. It is amazing how God can bless us with so much in our lives. Think for a moment of some of the blessings He has given you.

Delight yourself in the LORD and he will give you the desires of your heart.
(Psalm 37:4)

GROWING EGGHEADS

This wacky garden concoction is sure to plant a smile on your face. This is a great way to recycle used eggshells into little decorated homes for plants, herbs, flowers, or grass. We can learn about planting, watering, and caring for our little garden friends as we watch the miracle of growth.

WHAT YOU WILL NEED:

Eggs (pasteurized)
Potting soil
Grass seed, flower seeds, or herb seeds
Felt-tip markers

HOW TO CONCOCT IT:

1. Have an adult hollow out the eggs by tapping the small end against a hard surface to create a 1-inch hole on top of the egg.
2. Remove the contents of each egg by shaking it over a bowl.
3. Draw a face on your egghead using felt-tip markers.
4. Spoon each egg full of potting soil.
5. Make a small hole in the soil with a pencil.
6. Place a few seeds in the hole, cover with soil, and water it.
7. Depending on the type of seeds used, your Eggheads will sprout in 7 to 10 days.

CONCOCTION TIPS & IDEAS:

◆ By transplanting your Growing Eggheads outside, you can enjoy them all summer long.
◆ You can decorate little scenes on the eggs, write names on them, Scriptures, or fun drawings.
◆ As we care for our Eggheads, we are reminded that God created the plants for us to care for and to provide us with food. He also created grass and grains to feed many of the creatures He created.

He makes
grass grow for the cattle,
and plants for man to cultivate—
bringing forth food from the earth.
(Psalm 104:14)

FUNNY-FACE TOAST

Create funny faces, pictures, and designs that will brighten up your morning toast and put a smile on your face. God's Word tells us that when our hearts are delighted and happy, it shows on our face.

WHAT YOU WILL NEED:

2 Tbs. milk
Food coloring
Paintbrush
Slice of bread

HOW TO CONCOCT IT:

1. Mix milk and 2 drops of food coloring together in a small dish.
2. Use a paintbrush to paint a face or design on the slice of bread.
3. Toast the bread in a toaster set on the light setting.

CONCOCTION TIPS & IDEAS:

◆ Funny-Face Toast is great when used to make peanut butter and jelly or a BLT sandwich.
◆ This is a cool way to bring a little piece of joy to your daily routine. In one extra moment, breakfast can be filled with just a little more joy by creating Funny-Face Toast for someone you care about. As you go through your day, think of ways God can use you to give someone a happy heart.

A happy heart makes the face cheerful.
(Proverbs 15:13)

HEAVENLY CLOUD MARSHMALLOWS

Once you taste these old-fashioned, homemade treats, you'll never want store-bought marshmallows again. These marshmallows look like fluffy white clouds and remind us of the heavens above.

WHAT YOU WILL NEED:

1/4 cup water
4 Tbs. unflavored gelatin
2 1/2 cups sugar
3/4 cup light corn syrup
1 tsp. vanilla extract
Powdered sugar

HOW TO CONCOCT IT:

1. Mix the water, gelatin, sugar, corn syrup, and vanilla extract together in a pot.
2. Have an adult place the pot on the stove over medium-low heat, constantly stirring until the mixture is completely dissolved.
3. Remove from heat and pour the mixture into a 9 x 9 baking pan.
4. Place the pan in the refrigerator for 2 hours.
5. Cut the marshmallows into squares and dust with powdered sugar.

> In the beginning God created the heavens and the earth.
> (Genesis 1:1)

CONCOCTION TIPS & IDEAS:

◆ You can create yellow star marshmallows, great Christmas trees, red hearts, and more. Just add 10 to 12 drops of food coloring to the mixture in step 1. Then cut the chilled marshmallows into various shapes using cookie cutters.

◆ As you serve your Heavenly Cloud Marshmallows, read aloud from the book of Genesis. Discuss how God created the heavens and the earth in six days as you add each of the six ingredients in this concoction.

GOD'S COMPASS

This fun compass contraption always points to the north. God uses compass directions to explain to us why He removes our sins far from us when we are forgiven.

WHAT YOU WILL NEED:

Sewing needle
Magnet
Tape
Wide, flat piece of cork
Plate filled with water

HOW TO CONCOCT IT:

1. Magnetize the needle by stroking it with a magnet repeatedly in the same direction.
2. Tape the needle to the center of the cork.
3. Float the cork in the center of the water-filled plate.
4. The needle will always point north and south.

CONCOCTION TIPS & IDEAS:

◆ Create a portable compass by floating the cork and the needle in a shallow plastic glass.
◆ In His wisdom, God created the magnetic poles of the earth. With a compass we can tell if we are heading east or west, north or south. The Bible serves as a compass to tell us whether our lives are headed in the right direction.
◆ God tells us that as far as the east is from the west, He will remove our sins from our lives. We know this is far because the east and the west are in opposite directions. God is faithful to forgive us when we confess our sins to Him and follow His ways.

As far as the east is from the west, so far has he removed our transgressions from us.
(Psalm 103:12)

STAINED GLASS LAMP

This sun-and-moon Stained Glass Lamp represents the promise that God will always be with us, our children, our grandchildren, and all future generations.

WHAT YOU WILL NEED:

4 oz. white glue
4 oz. water
Blue, orange, and yellow tissue paper
Glass baby food jar (clean with the label removed)
Paintbrush

HOW TO CONCOCT IT:

1. Mix water and white glue together in a small bowl to create your stained glass adhesive.
2. Cut a small moon shape out of the yellow tissue paper and a sun shape out of the orange tissue paper.
3. Using a paintbrush, cover the baby food jar with the adhesive mixture. Place the sun on one side of the jar and the moon shape on the opposite side.
4. Fill the rest of the adhesive covered space on the jar with small torn or cut pieces of blue tissue paper.
5. Place a small battery-operated light in the jar or have an adult place a tea candle in the center of the jar.

CONCOCTION TIPS & IDEAS:

◆ Make your jar look like leaded stained glass by outlining the pieces of tissue with a medium-tip black tip marker.
.◆ The Bible tells us that God will be with us forever and that He will never leave us or forsake us.

He will endure as long as the sun, as long as the moon, through all generations.
(Psalm 72:5)

CHOCOLATE SMOOCHES

Our giant Chocolate Smooches taste great, and when eaten as a special treat, they make us feel happy inside. These giant Smooches also make great gifts. You can even add your favorite Scripture to this delicious treat to make the gift more meaningful.

WHAT YOU WILL NEED:

1 bag of milk-chocolate chips
Round kitchen funnel
Coffee mug
Nonstick cooking spray
Aluminum foil

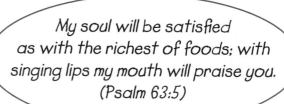

HOW TO CONCOCT IT:

1. Have an adult melt the chocolate chips in a double broiler or in a microwave.

2. Block the small end of the funnel up with a wad of aluminum foil.

3. Place the funnel upright in a coffee mug. Spray the funnel with cooking spray.

4. Pour the melted chocolate into the funnel and place it in the freezer for 2 hours or until the chocolate has hardened completely.

5. Remove the chocolate from the funnel and wrap in aluminum foil.

6. Write a message or Scripture on a small narrow strip of paper and tuck in into the foil at the end of your Chocolate Smooch.

CONCOCTION TIPS & IDEAS:

◆ You can drizzle your milk Chocolate Smooch with white chocolate or make White Chocolate Smooches drizzled with milk chocolate. Our children love to layer different colors of chocolate to create rainbow-color Smooches.

◆ The book of Psalms tells us that as we grow to love and know God more, our souls will feel happy and satisfied—so much that we will want to sing from our hearts songs that express to God how much we love and worship Him. Just as we give the gift of chocolate to someone we care for, we can give God the gift of our love and worship.

> My soul will be satisfied as with the richest of foods; with singing lips my mouth will praise you. (Psalm 63:5)

POPCORN TREASURE BALLS

These tasty popcorn balls have a hidden treasure treat in the center. God also has hidden treasure for those of us who seek to find it. Only God can give us these treasures through His understanding and wisdom.

WHAT YOU WILL NEED:

2 cups plain popped popcorn

1/2 cup corn syrup

1/2 cup sugar

Butter

Edible treasures (ring pops, candy necklaces, gummy bears, etc.)

HOW TO CONCOCT IT:

1. Have an adult combine sugar and corn syrup in a pot and cook over medium heat until the sugar is completely dissolved.

2. Let the sugar mixture completely cool.

3. Pour the sugar mixture evenly over the popcorn.

4. Butter your hands and form a popcorn ball around the edible treasure..

CONCOCTION TIPS & IDEAS:

◆ Add a handful of Nerds candy to the sugar-and-popcorn mixture for a burst of color and flavor.

◆ Just as we search the popcorn ball with excitement to find the candy treasures inside, God wants us to seek Him with excitement. He promises that if we do, we will find the knowledge and understanding only He can give.

If you look for it as for silver and search for it as for hidden treasure, then you will understand the fear of the LORD and find the knowledge of God.
(Proverbs 2:4-5)

Index

TOY CONCOCTIONS

Miracle Art Board.............................22
Word Cannon....................................24
Hydro Jet Ark..................................36
Splongee Ball of Virtues.................44
Heavenly Treasures Bottle...............45
Water Balloon Yo-Yo 47
David's Slingshot Flyer...................52

DOUGH

Treasure Stones.............................10
Fruit of the Spirit Dough.................12
Cinnamon Heart Ornaments............54
Surprise Soaps...............................64

GARDEN CONCOCTIONS

Mini Garden of Eden 15
Grass Hair Guy 16
Living Basket...................................38
Flower Transfers 41
Living Words 42
Growing Eggheads..........................66

PAINTS

Promise of the Rainbow Paint..............11
Bubbling Peace Paint.......................21
Marble Paint..................................26
Heavenly Cloud Paint 27
Bubble Paint...................................49
Super Sidewalk Paint 51
Washable Window Art 55
Ten Commandments Paint Pens.............58
Shower Time Paints........................60
Beautiful-in-Time Marbleizing.............61

EDIBLE CONCOCTIONS

Dog and Cat Treats........................13
Romans Ice Cream..........................28
"No Worry" Bird Cookies 33
Edible Ocean in a Bag....................34
Jiggle Orange Slices.......................56
Holiday Peppermint Wreaths............62
Shake-and-Make Slushy 63
Spaghetti Ice Cream Sundae................65
Funny-Face Toast 67
Heavenly Cloud Marshmallows............68
Chocolate Smooches 71

Popcorn Treasure Balls 72
Manna Dessert 75

PUTTY & CLAY

Gooey Creation Gunk.............................20
Divine Dryer Lint Clay............................46
Moses' Miracle Muck..............................53
Super Bubble Slime.................................57

CANDLES & LANTERNS

Sparkle Lamp...14
Sparkling Glitter Candles.........................40
Stained Glass Lamp 70
Pathway Lanterns....................................73

OTHER CONCOCTIONS

Fizzle Stones 17
Storm in a Bottle.....................................18
Power of Prayer Rain Stick......................19
Phony Spill...23
Scents of Joy 29
Resurrection Sand Eggs...........................30
Honey Lip Balm..32
Friendship Stone......................................35
Color-Change Bath Salts.........................39

Creation Sand Plaques 43
World's Best Bubbles 48
Scripture Sidewalk Chalk 50
God's Compass 69
Surging Sea Lamp...................................74

John & Danita Thomas

Never hear the words "Mom, I'm bored" again!

What do you get when you take one bored child and add used coffee grounds, dryer lint, and Elmer's Glue? No, it's not your worst nightmare — it's a recipe for fun!

In fact, Kid Concoctions is a mom's dream come true!

Now you can use common household ingredients to entertain (and educate) the entire family. Each Kid Concoctions collection contains dozens of easy-to-make projects that rival toy store products in quality and cost just pennies.

"Top-secret recipes toy manufacturers pray you will never learn." — Parent Soup

"Entertain the kids and save money. Half the fun is in the making." — NBC News

"With these resources your children will never be bored again." — Stevanne "Dr. Toy" Auerbach

"It's like sneaking a peek at classified FBI spy files. A frugal parent's dream come true." — Moms Online

"Hours of absorbed, lively, creative fun and inspiration for a lifetime of imaginative endeavors." — Amazon.com

The Ultimate Book of Holiday Kid Concoctions
ISBN-10: 0-8054-4445-9
The Ultimate Book of Kid Concoctions
ISBN-10: 0-8054-4443-2
The Ultimate Book of Kid Concoctions 2
ISBN-10: 0-8054-4444-0
Kid Concoctions & Contraptions
ISBN-10: 0-8054-4446-7

Available at your local bookstore
or call 1.800.233.1123 today!

www.kidconcoctions.com

www.bhpublishinggroup.com

b&h
Kids

PATHWAY LANTERNS

Pathway Lanterns will not only light your way in style; they will remind you that God tells us if we follow His Word and obey His commandments, our paths will be much clearer.

WHAT YOU WILL NEED:

Soup can (clean with label removed)
Hammer
Nail
Paper
Battery -operated light or votive candle
Tape

HOW TO CONCOCT IT:

1. Fill the soup can with water and place in the freezer for 24 hours until frozen solid.
2. Cut a piece of paper the same size as the height and diameter of the can.
3. Use a pencil to draw a simple basic design on the paper (e.g., a cross, star, heart, or snowflake).
4. Remove the can from the freezer and secure the design around the can with a piece of tape.
5. Lay the can on a thick, folded towel and ask an adult to help you use the hammer and a nail to punch holes along the lines of the design.
6. Place the can in warm water until the ice is melted.
7. Place a battery-operated light or votive candle inside the dry can.

CONCOCTION TIPS & IDEAS:

◆ Pathway Lanterns can be used outside for birthday parties or holiday celebrations.
◆ These lanterns will light up the path on the ground so we can see where to walk in the dark. When we lose our way in darkness, God will light the path and help us get back on track. He gives us wisdom to live a good life that will honor Him and bless us.

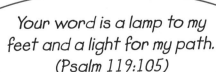

Your word is a lamp to my feet and a light for my path. (Psalm 119:105)

SURGING SEA LAMP

This bubbling concoction of water and oil looks like a 1970s lava lamp, but it is a colorful reminder of God's power over the earth and its elements. Even after God created the heavens and the earth, He performed many miracles showing His power among His people.

WHAT YOU WILL NEED:

Cooking oil

Kosher salt

Blue food coloring

Water

Clear plastic or glass jar (e.g., an empty peanut butter jar, clean
   with the label removed)

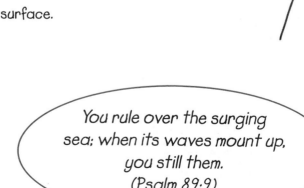

HOW TO CONCOCT IT:

1. Fill the jar 3/4 full with water and add 4 to 6 drops of food coloring.
2. Fill the jar almost to the top with cooking oil. Give the mixture a few minutes
   to settle and allow the liquid to completely separate.
3. Sprinkle a small handful of kosher salt on top of the oil. The salt pulls some of
   the oil to the bottom of the jar. When the salt dissolves, the oil comes back to the surface.
   This creates the bubbling seawater effect.
4. Add more salt and your Surging Sea Lamp will start to bubble all over again.

CONCOCTION TIPS & IDEAS:

◆ Use red or green food coloring to create a Lava Lamp or Slime Lamp.
◆ As we learn more about God and His amazing miracles, we soon realize that there
   isn't anything God cannot do. Jesus said, "All things are possible with God"
   (Mark 10:27).

You rule over the surging sea; when its waves mount up, you still them.
(Psalm 89:9)

MANNA DESSERT

Manna Dessert is a tasty after-supper treat that reminds us of the food that God sent from the skies of heaven to feed His chosen people. This concoction is a great way to spark mealtime conversation about the many things God has given us that we should be thankful for.

WHAT YOU WILL NEED:

1 cup vanilla pudding

1/2 cup crushed vanilla wafers

HOW TO CONCOCT IT:

1. Spoon the vanilla pudding into a clear cup or glass.
2. Sprinkle the crushed vanilla wafers on top of the pudding. This looks like the pieces of manna from heaven.

CONCOCTION TIPS & IDEAS:

◆ Have fun by making your Manna Dessert look like a mini-beach. Add a small drink umbrella and a couple of round, colored candies to look like beach balls.

◆ Let everyone make their own raining of the manna by sprinkling their crushed wafers on top of the dessert. Imagine how the children of Israel must have felt so thankful and full of faith as their food just rained down out of the sky.

> Yet he gave a command to the skies above and opened the doors of the heavens; he rained down manna for the people to eat, he gave them the grain of heaven.
> (Psalm 78:23–24)

Index

TOY CONCOCTIONS

Miracle Art Board.............................22
Word Cannon.................................24
Hydro Jet Ark...............................36
Splongee Ball of Virtues...................44
Heavenly Treasures Bottle..................45
Water Balloon Yo-Yo 47
David's Slingshot Flyer....................52

DOUGH

Treasure Stones............................10
Fruit of the Spirit Dough..................12
Cinnamon Heart Ornaments 54
Surprise Soaps.............................64

GARDEN CONCOCTIONS

Mini Garden of Eden 15
Grass Hair Guy 16
Living Basket..............................38
Flower Transfers 41
Living Words 42
Growing Eggheads...........................66

PAINTS

Promise of the Rainbow Paint...............11
Bubbling Peace Paint.......................21
Marble Paint...............................26
Heavenly Cloud Paint 27
Bubble Paint...............................49
Super Sidewalk Paint 51
Washable Window Art 55
Ten Commandments Paint Pens 58
Shower Time Paints.........................60
Beautiful-in-Time Marbleizing..............61

EDIBLE CONCOCTIONS

Dog and Cat Treats 13
Romans Ice Cream 28
"No Worry" Bird Cookies 33
Edible Ocean in a Bag 34
Jiggle Orange Slices.......................56
Holiday Peppermint Wreaths.................62
Shake-and-Make Slushy 63
Spaghetti Ice Cream Sundae.................65
Funny-Face Toast 67
Heavenly Cloud Marshmallows................68
Chocolate Smooches 71

Popcorn Treasure Balls 72
Manna Dessert 75

PUTTY & CLAY

Gooey Creation Gunk 20
Divine Dryer Lint Clay 46
Moses' Miracle Muck 53
Super Bubble Slime 57

CANDLES & LANTERNS

Sparkle Lamp..14
Sparkling Glitter Candles......................40
Stained Glass Lamp 70
Pathway Lanterns.................................73

OTHER CONCOCTIONS

Fizzle Stones 17
Storm in a Bottle 18
Power of Prayer Rain Stick....................19
Phony Spill...23
Scents of Joy 29
Resurrection Sand Eggs........................30
Honey Lip Balm....................................32
Friendship Stone..................................35
Color-Change Bath Salts......................39

Creation Sand Plaques 43
World's Best Bubbles 48
Scripture Sidewalk Chalk 50
God's Compass 69
Surging Sea Lamp.................................74

John & Danita Thomas

Never hear the words "Mom, I'm bored" again!

What do you get when you take one bored child and add used coffee grounds, dryer lint, and Elmer's Glue? No, it's not your worst nightmare — it's a recipe for fun!

In fact, Kid Concoctions is a mom's dream come true!

Now you can use common household ingredients to entertain (and educate) the entire family. Each Kid Concoctions collection contains dozens of easy-to-make projects that rival toy store products in quality and cost just pennies.

"Top-secret recipes toy manufacturers pray you will never learn." — Parent Soup

"Entertain the kids and save money. Half the fun is in the making." — NBC News

"With these resources your children will never be bored again." — Stevanne "Dr. Toy" Auerbach

"It's like sneaking a peek at classified FBI spy files. A frugal parent's dream come true." — Moms Online

"Hours of absorbed, lively, creative fun and inspiration for a lifetime of imaginative endeavors." — Amazon.com

The Ultimate Book of Holiday Kid Concoctions
ISBN-10: 0-8054-4445-9
The Ultimate Book of Kid Concoctions
ISBN-10: 0-8054-4443-2
The Ultimate Book of Kid Concoctions 2
ISBN-10: 0-8054-4444-0
Kid Concoctions & Contraptions
ISBN-10: 0-8054-4446-7

Available at your local bookstore or call 1.800.233.1123 today!

www.kidconcoctions.com

www.bhpublishinggroup.com

b&h Kids